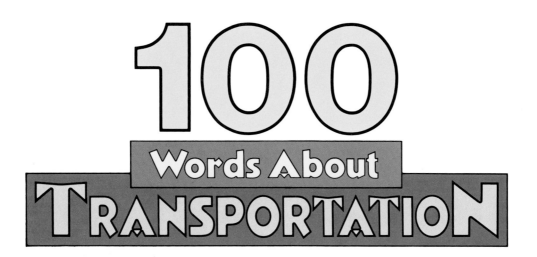

100 Words About
Words About
TRANSPORTATION

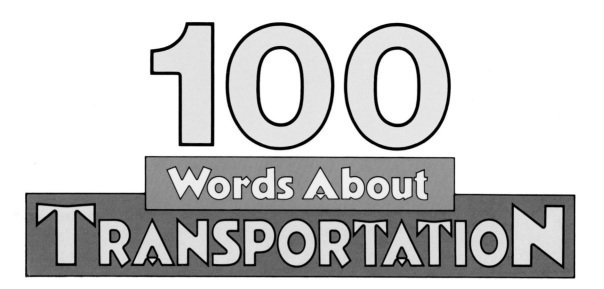

100 Words About TRANSPORTATION

Illustrated by Richard Brown

HBJ

Gulliver Books
Harcourt Brace Jovanovich
San Diego   Austin   Orlando

Requests for permission to make copies of any
part of the work should be mailed to:
Permissions, Harcourt Brace Jovanovich, Publishers,
Orlando, Florida 32887.

Library of Congress Cataloging-in-Publication Data
100 words about transportation.
''Gulliver books.''
Summary: Labeled illustrations present 100 words about
transportation, arranged by concepts such as ''In the
Water,'' ''In Distant Lands,'' and ''In an Emergency.''
1. Transportation—Terminology—Juvenile literature.
2. Transportation—Pictorial works—Juvenile literature.
3. Picture dictionaries, English—Juvenile literature.
[1. Transportation—Pictorial works. 2. Vocabulary]
I. Brown, Richard Eric, 1946–   ill. II. Title: One
hundred words about transportation.
HE152.A114 1987   380.5′014   86-22781
ISBN 0-15-200551-X

Designed by G.B.D. Smith
Printed and bound by Tien Wah (PTE.) Ltd. Lithographers, Singapore.
A B C D E
First edition

To Lynne

—R.B.

walk

skip

hop

roll

run

crawl

tricycle

unicycle

bicycle

scooter

skateboard

wagon

roller skates

IN THE CITY

trolley

BUS

59 A

bus

subway

82 W

limousine

wheelchair

stroller

taxi

tractor

pickup truck

horse

train

horse trailer

school bus

garbage truck

moving van

tugboat

cement mixer

pushcart

truck

car

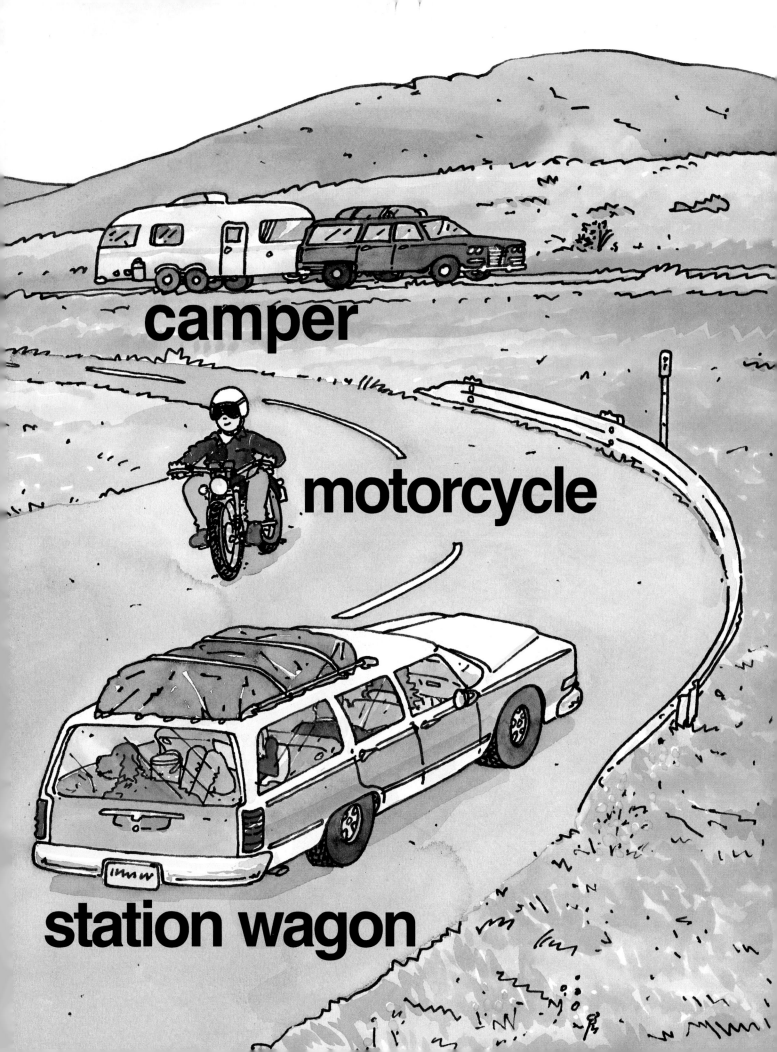

camper

motorcycle

station wagon

submarine

canoe

rowboat

raft

ocean liner

yacht

motorboat

sailboat

sleigh

snowmobile

ice skates

snowplow

chair lift

skis

sled

helicopter

jet

airplane

parachute

blimp

hang glider

balloon

rocket ship

space shuttle

spacecraft

elephant

camel

donkey

dogsled

rickshaw

IN THE PAST

steamboat

litter

chariot

stagecoach

cart

carriage

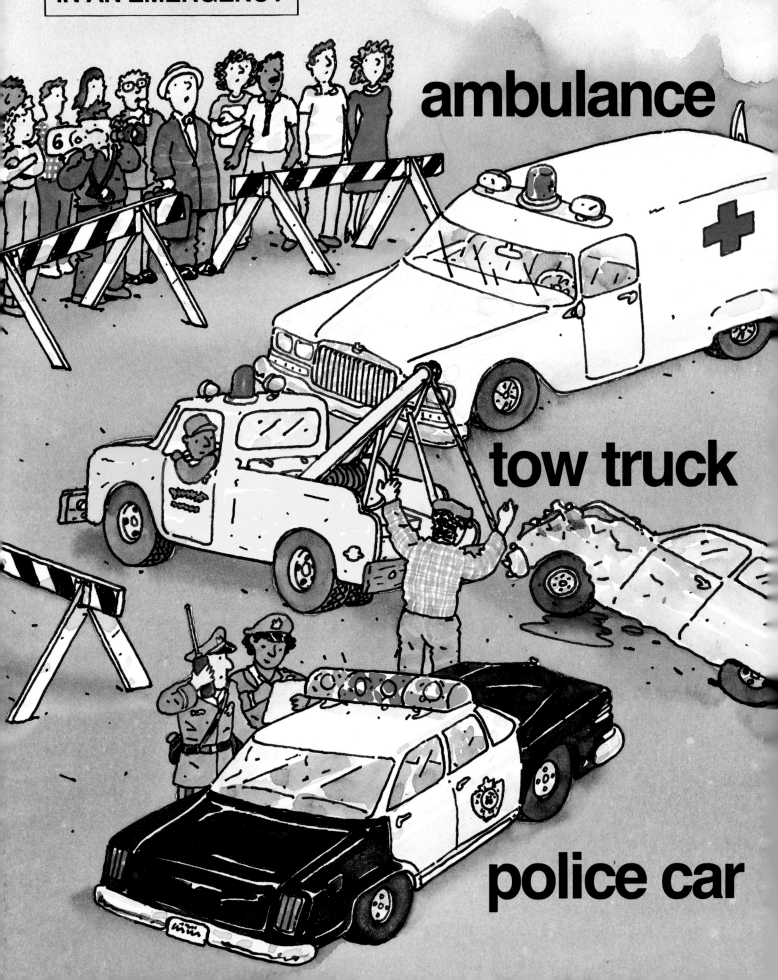

IN AN EMERGENCY

ambulance

tow truck

police car

fire truck

AT AN AMUSEMENT PARK

roller coaster

merry-go-round

monorail

tramway

Ferris wheel